About Demos

Who we are

Demos is the think tank for everyday democracy. We believe everyone should be able to make personal choices in their daily lives that contribute to the common good. Our aim is to put this democratic idea into practice by working with organisations in ways that make them more effective and legitimate.

What we work on

We focus on six areas: public services; science and technology; cities and public space; people and communities; arts and culture; and global security.

Who we work with

Our partners include policy-makers, companies, public service providers and social entrepreneurs. Demos is not linked to any party but we work with politicians across political divides. Our international network – which extends across Eastern Europe, Scandinavia, Australia, Brazil, India and China – provides a global perspective and enables us to work across borders.

How we work

Demos knows the importance of learning from experience. We test and improve our ideas in practice by working with people who can make change happen. Our collaborative approach means that our partners share in the creation and ownership of new ideas.

What we offer

We analyse social and political change, which we connect to innovation and learning in organisations. We help our partners show thought leadership and respond to emerging policy challenges.

How we communicate

As an independent voice, we can create debates that lead to real change. We use the media, public events, workshops and publications to communicate our ideas. All our books can be downloaded free from the Demos website.

www.demos.co.uk

First published in 2006
© Demos
Some rights reserved – see copyright licence for details

ISBN 1 84180 168 2
Typeset by utimestwo, Collingtree, Northants
Printed by Iprint, Leicester

For further information and
subscription details please contact:

Demos
Magdalen House
136 Tooley Street
London SE1 2TU

telephone: 0845 458 5949
email: hello@demos.co.uk
web: www.demos.co.uk

Not a Sideshow: Leadership and Cultural Value

A matrix for change

Robert Hewison

Supported by

CALOUSTE
GULBENKIAN
FOUNDATION

DEM⊙S

DEM⊙S

Contents

"As people begin to use a different language to describe what they do, they tend to change what they see and do."
Mark H. Moore, *Creating Public Value*, (1995)[1]

Acknowledgements

In his recent Demos essay, *Talk Us Into It*, Samuel Jones calls for a revival in the art of conversation. I could not agree with him more, for without the conversations that have developed around the idea of Cultural Value, this new essay would not have been possible. My friend and colleague at Demos, John Holden, has led the discussion, as my introduction makes clear, and Charlie Tims and Samuel Jones at Demos have helpfully joined in. Kate Clark and Liz Forgan at the Heritage Lottery Fund have materially helped with the development of the discourse of Cultural Value, and I have had useful exchanges with Adrian Ellis, David Throsby, Ricardo Blaug and Sally Bacon. I would also like to thank the Clore Fellows Andrew Missingham and Stephen Escritt for sharing their views, and Sara Selwood, Head of the Department of Cultural Policy and Management at City University, together with Judith Palmer, Caroline Thornbury and Claire Whitaker, participants in City's cultural leadership programme.

I would like to thank especially Paula Ridley and the staff of the United Kingdom branch of the Calouste Gulbenkian Foundation for their support not only of this publication, but of work that John Holden and I have been engaged with since 2004

Robert Hewiston
November 2006

Introduction

This essay builds on two previous Demos pamphlets written by my colleague John Holden, *Capturing Cultural Value* (2004) and *Cultural Value and the Crisis of Legitimacy* (2006), both of which set out to develop a more sophisticated way of expressing the totality of values that are associated with the enjoyment of culture generally, and the arts and heritage in particular. These essays have already begun to prove their worth as an aid to the development of public policy, as our work for the Heritage Lottery Fund has shown. But whereas the previous two Demos pamphlets concentrated on explaining how the many different valuations that can be placed on Culture could be expressed within the over-arching concept of Cultural Value, this latest contribution to the debate seeks to go further, by developing the idea of Cultural Value into a critical tool that can be used by cultural institutions to improve their professional practice, the services they deliver, and the value they create.

The essay suggests a new conceptual approach to the practice of cultural institutions and of the people who work in them. It therefore concentrates on one of the integral elements of Cultural Value, that is to say Institutional Value, and it argues that the adoption of Institutional Value as an analytical methodology will lead to positive organisational change. The context of the essay is the general recognition that the cultural sector needs to strengthen its leadership, emblematised by the government's decision to invest £12 million in enhancing the leadership skills of the sector. The application of the concepts associated with Institutional Value is proposed as a way by which a new approach to Leadership, and ultimately different organisational forms, will emerge.

The focus of the essay is on the publicly funded cultural sector, and includes the performing arts, libraries and archives, museums and galleries. It is concerned both with the organisations that present the manifestations of culture, and the bodies that set policy and give financial support. The sector exists within a mixed economy of public and private commercial interests, individuals and trusts, but because of the sense of purpose of the sector and those working in it, together with the role played by public subvention, it constitutes a vital part of the public, as distinguished from the commercial, realm. Yet, as people working in the sector are deeply aware, publicly funded culture does not enjoy the same political legitimacy afforded to education, health, law and order, defence or even sport. This has contributed to the crisis of leadership that the recent government initiative is intended to address.

At the same time, for a number of years, the values associated with aspects of the public realm, and not just culture, such as health, education, local democracy and transport have been under attack in the name of "efficiency", "modernisation" and "consumer choice". The concept of Cultural Value was developed in response to the distinctive situation and characteristics of the cultural sector, but many of the ideas are drawn from a larger debate about the role of institutions in the public realm, and the principles proposed could be applied in that wider sphere.

1. "Not a sideshow"

At 7.30 a.m. on the morning on 20th June 2006 a group of leading figures in the world of the arts, museums and galleries gathered in what were for them the unfamiliar surroundings of the Chancellor of the Exchequer's reception rooms at No 11 Downing Street. They were there to hear Gordon Brown formally launch a two-year programme to improve the management and leadership of the cultural sector. Bypassing the Department for Culture, Media and Sport, he had entrusted £12 million jointly to Arts Council England, the Museums, Libraries and Archives Council and the sector's skills council, Creative and Cultural Skills, to devise a series of programmes to hone the talents of high-flyers in the cultural sector, and to promote the emergence of a more diverse group of cultural leaders. Some 2,000 people are expected to benefit from the variety of imaginative training and personal development schemes that are now being put in place.

The cultural sector has rarely been either consistently or adequately funded, whatever party has been in power. The total spending of the Department for Culture, Media and Sport has never exceeded 0.34% of total government expenditure. In his early morning speech, however, the Chancellor was emphatic about his commitment to this new project:

> *What we are talking about this morning is something that is not at the margins, but in the mainstream now. It is not a sideshow, it is right at the centre – not just of a modern culture and a modern society, but of a modern economy.*

The reference to the economy was deliberate. Politicians have come to understand that the cultural sector is a key driver of the creative industries, which are growing at a much faster rate than the economy as a whole. The Chancellor was happy to cite Sir George Cox's 2005 review of creativity in business, which reports that the sector contributes 8% of gross added value to the national economy, and is worth £11.5 billion to the balance of trade.[2] Gordon Brown wants more of this, and he believes that the arts may have something to teach the business world:

> *The learning of leadership skills and management skills is critically essential for our future and the encouragement that we are trying to give to an interaction between the arts and the business world will be of benefit I may say, not simply to you, in the cultural world but also to business itself who will learn from you.*

But what will the fortunate 2,000 learn – and what do they have to teach the business sector?

2. The Call for Leadership

Since the turn of the new century, Leadership has been seen as both the source of, and the solution to, the problems of the modern economy. If Leadership were a fashion colour, it would be the new black. The importance of Leadership has always been recognised, and it is acknowledged to be something different to management. It is seen as a set of behaviours that inspire members of an organisation to excel, as opposed to the skills they also need for that organisation to be able to deliver. The organisation might be an army, a church, or a widget factory, but good Leadership appears to be needed most in the commercial and public sector. The behaviour of certain business leaders, notably Jeffrey Skilling and his chairman Ken Lay at Enron in the United States, has called into question the morality and style of business leadership as it was previously understood. Business schools in Britain are placing a renewed emphasis on improving commercial leadership, with courses and research centres explicitly focussed on Leadership at universities such as Exeter, Lancaster, the Cass Business School, City University and Royal Holloway College, London University. There is also a new emphasis on developing Leadership in education, the health sector and public administration generally.

The rapidity of economic change, the speed of communications and the shifting tides of global power, have placed a premium on successful Leadership. The followers of the ordered routines of management need to be told what it is that they have to deliver;

managers will perform better if there is someone who can communicate a forward vision that will encourage them to be flexible, productive and committed, and who can guide them through the rapid changes that the quickening pace of globalisation has brought about. Yet in spite of the existence of a prolific literature on Leadership, there is no common agreement as to what it is. The meaning of the word Leadership is almost as fiercely contested as that of the word Culture. Nonetheless $50 billion a year is currently being spent worldwide on leadership development.[3]

In the cultural sector until very recently, Leadership was thought of as something that emerged spontaneously, as part of the job. After all, there has been no shortage of charismatic and creative people, from Diaghilev to Sir Peter Hall, who have stamped their personalities on arts organisations. This approach to Leadership was consonant with an attitude that the 1997 Holland Report, *Review of Management Training and Development in the Museums, Galleries and Heritage Sector* called "the Culture of Professionalism".[4] Professional subject expertise – be it curatorial scholarship or creative flair as an artistic director – was more highly valued than the ordinary management skills associated with the efficient running of an organisation. Then, around the turn of the new century, Britain's cultural sector saw a series of spectacular crises in important organisations, beginning with the Royal Opera House in 1997-8, followed by the Royal Shakespeare Company, English National Opera, and the British Museum in 2001-2. None of these organisations collapsed, and there was no suggestion of the venality that infected Enron, but the solution to these crises – apart from large injections of money – was believed to be renewed Leadership, as a series of reports, following on from Holland, testified.[5] At that time the only cultural leadership course available in the United Kingdom was a two-week summer Museum Leadership Course, launched in 1994 and open to about a dozen people, at the University of East Anglia.

In 2002 Dame Vivien Duffield, who as chair of the Clore Duffield Foundation is a significant patron of the arts (and therefore has an informed view of the possible deficiencies of cultural organisations) decided to address the acknowledged Leadership deficit, and the Clore Leadership Programme was launched in 2003. The programme, which is also offering new short courses as part of the Treasury's national Cultural Leadership Programme, gives a highly bespoke training to between 25 and 30 people a year, at an approximate cost of £55,000 each. In July 2006, funded by the European Community's Social Fund, the Cultural Policy and Management Department at City University launched the first academically accredited course in Cultural Leadership, restricted, in its first year, to women only, with 48 accepted to take part.

There are now some 75 Clore Fellows, men and women, who have completed the course or are currently in the system. As the national Cultural Leadership Programme comes on stream, there will be at least 2000 more people prepared to take up enhanced leadership positions. In a sector that is variously calculated to employ between 650,000 and 1.8 million people,[6] there is no danger that we will run out of followers, but there remains a question to be asked, not about the wisdom of investing in cultural Leadership, but as to how effectively this welcome investment can be exploited.

Whatever the particular style of Leadership that is inculcated (and there are a number to choose from), leaders have been seen as distinct from the organisations they lead, and to date Leadership training has tended to focus on the development of the individual. She or he is introduced to certain behaviours that are believed to produce effective Leadership, and encouraged to back this up with the acquisition of the necessary management skills that will help to translate inspired mission into effective execution.

Beneficiaries of Leadership training report the life-changing effect of the experience of being encouraged to see themselves as leaders. But they also describe the difficulties they encounter when, fresh from their Leadership training, they return, changed, to the unchanged organisations and cultural landscape from which they come. Some solve the problem by moving to other organisations, which can leave their former employer disgruntled at the loss of an employee whose value they had recognised by sending them for Leadership training in the first place. Others simply become frustrated, and their sense of personal empowerment fades.

In short, it seems that there is only limited benefit to be derived from changing an individual, if institutions remain unchanged. The leadership crises at the turn of the century did not produce significant structural change. It requires a larger effort than most single individuals can produce to turn round an institution, even if the cult of charismatic Leadership suggests that he or she can. It requires collective as well as individual effort to change the culture of an organisation. What is needed is a critical tool that will help leaders *and* their institutions effect the changes that are needed to make the investment of £12 million worthwhile.

3. The Business of Culture and the Culture of Business

It is reassuring to discover that Gordon Brown believes that business can learn from the cultural sector, but it is important to recognise that the creativity and innovation that he wishes to capture happens in a very different environment to that of business. True, the cultural sector, and its surrounding penumbra, the creative industries, operate in a market economy and can be highly entrepreneurial, but when we look at the operation of the economics of the arts, we find that conditions are often determined not by the invisible hand of the market, but by its opposite, market failure.

Market failure occurs when it proves impossible to produce certain goods in sufficient quantity and/or at an acceptable price to justify their existence in purely monetary terms. In particular the market fails to produce, or under-produces, cultural goods such as dance, symphony orchestras and new political plays, and it is difficult to protect desirable landscape or historic properties from the depredations of developers. The arts are particularly susceptible to market failure because they are unable – outside books, film and recordings – to reproduce their creations in sufficient numbers to exploit their success beyond a certain level. Nor can the arts easily achieve economies of scale. You cannot downsize an orchestra, nor can you upscale an auditorium without radically altering the audience experience.

A cold-hearted answer to this problem would be to say that the market cannot supply these things because there is insufficient demand for them. But that is not the case. There is demand of a different kind: national or local prestige, a belief in the educational value of the arts and heritage, a belief in the morally redemptive power of culture are implicit or explicit reasons for wanting to have these things. So the visible hand of patronage reaches in. The market has to be altered by regulation – as in the case of zoning green belt land and listing heritage properties – or by state or private philanthropy that ensures through subsidy that there is a sufficient supply of what are deemed to be socially necessary cultural goods – one of them being that will-o-the-wisp, "creativity".

Cultural life, in its broadest sense, is not defined by the existence of public subsidy, although it is conditioned by it. It is obvious that some kind of cultural activity will take place whether there is public intervention or not, and it is also true that public and private patronage will happen whether or not there is market failure, because culture is believed to be desirable regardless of market forces. But the fact that, in general, cultural goods *are* judged to be socially necessary, as opposed to widgets, which are economically necessary, plays into the fundamental difference between the business of culture and the culture of business. Although private commercial enterprises have an important role in the cultural sector, particularly in the field of entertainment – the term is used non-pejoratively – a key difference between culture and business is that businesses have shareholders, and cultural organisations have stakeholders.

True, commercial companies have to consider government regulators, their workforce and the communities in which they operate, but the shareholder is the driver. In *The Culture of the New Capitalism* Richard Sennett, Professor of Sociology at the London School of Economics, argues that there has been an important shift in shareholder attitudes that has destabilised the culture of business and contributed to the crisis of Leadership that is our present context. Whereas previously shareholders, as individuals or institutions, were primarily interested in their annual dividends, the creation of new financial instruments and the internationalisation of commerce has shifted attention to share-price: "short-term rather than long-term results".[7]

Sennett coins the striking phrase "institutional beauty" to explain the pressure companies like Enron were under to appear attractive to the market at all times: "institutional beauty consisted in demonstrating signs of internal change and flexibility, appearing to be a dynamic company, even if the once-stable company had worked perfectly well".[8] Being focussed on the short-term, commercial firms will have little, if any, concern for the effect that what they do will have on future generations, whereas institutions in the public sphere which receive taxpayers' money take on longer term responsibilities in return. The reason for drawing attention to this organisational restlessness is that it has also begun to affect the public sector, in the guise of "modernisation". All three of the organisations responsible for delivering the national Cultural Leadership Programme, Arts Council England, the Museums, Libraries and Archives Council and Creative and Cultural Skills have undergone recent reorganisation. Paradoxically, "change" has become a constant.

Since, by and large then, cultural organisations do not have shareholders, it follows that they do not produce financial dividends: rather, as will be argued in a moment, they produce dividends of a different kind. The power of stakeholders is expressed in far more complicated ways than share price. Such are the contradictory interests of cultural stakeholders that one group may be eager to sell because of circumstances that make another group eager to buy.

The primary, most important, stakeholders are those working in the cultural organisation itself. It is their creative vision that has made it what it is, and they have often taken risks and accepted low material rewards to achieve their creative or curatorial ambitions. But their aspirations may well not harmonise easily with those of the one or more public bodies upon which they depend for financial support, who as a result of the developments in cultural policy since the 1980s will have a social and/or economic agenda to consider as well as a cultural one. It is also the case that the interests of local and national funding bodies are rarely the same. Such is the need for commercial sponsorship, for help from charitable foundations and from private patrons, these too, with their individual interests, are also eagerly brought on board. Also in the mix is the audience, by no means a homogenous group but one that ranges from volunteers to Friends' organisations to professional critics to occasional punters, all of whose views will have influence. At one remove, people who may have no connection with the organisation or its work at all may have an interest, if only as tax payers, in the organisation's existence.

"Institutional beauty" therefore has a different meaning in the cultural sector, and it is arguable that such are the conflicting interests of their multifarious stakeholders, the job of cultural leaders is even more difficult than that of business chief executives. As participants in the public realm, they have to recognise that they operate in a political environment, usually with a small, but sometimes with a big, P. The difficulty for those in the cultural sector, however, is that unlike other features of the public realm such as health or education, there is no generally perceived "right" to culture. People do feel entitled to health care and education, but notwithstanding Article 27 of the United Nations Declaration of Human Rights the claim of culture to merit public support is still contested.[9]

The "dividend" produced by a cultural organisation is the work it does in meeting the needs of its stakeholders. This begins with the artistic imperatives of those inside the organisation, but it extends to the far wider social and economic benefits that are to be derived from having a successful cultural organisation (or even a single artist) in the vicinity. The dividend can be viewed as tangible – for instance as a contribution to urban regeneration or tourist revenue – or as intangible: local or national pride in the organisation, as a symbol of local or national identity, as a stimulus to people's creativity, imagination and sense of wellbeing. People working in the subsidised cultural sector – in common with people working in education or health – believe that they are adding to the country's store of social capital, that they are improving the public realm. By encouraging people to engage in common cultural interests they are strengthening civic society and putting something back, as opposed to merely taking things out. The public realm is used for leisure and pleasure, but it is also where people become citizens, not just consumers. An opinion poll cited by the Cabinet Office Strategy Unit showed: "66% of people referred to their relationship with public services as being that of citizens or members of the public compared to only 30% who thought of themselves as customers or users".[10] The culture of business, on the other hand, makes people eager to privatise the public realm, and thinks less in terms of common good than competing individual appetites to be profitably exploited.

In the light of what is to follow, it must also be pointed out that the people who are ultimately responsible for producing a cultural dividend play a role that is quite different to that of the directors of a commercial company. Company directors rightly expect to share in the financial profits of the enterprises they lead: most cultural organisations, however, are charities, and board members are forbidden by law from benefiting financially from the organisations for which they are responsible. Their rewards are of another kind. Gratification of personal vanity may be one of them, but there is also the satisfaction of contributing to the common good.

None of this is intended to disappoint Gordon Brown in his hopes that the cultural sector may be able to transfer some of its creative skills to the world of business. But it is important to recognise that not only are these two spheres operating in different financial contexts, they ultimately have different values. Any enterprise may be concerned about its institutional beauty, but what is important for an organisation in the cultural sector is its Institutional Value.

4. Cultural Value

This essay builds on the work of John Holden in developing the theory of Cultural Value in two earlier Demos publications, *Capturing Cultural Value* (2004) and *Cultural Value and the Crisis of Legitimacy* (2006).[11] In the first of these he set out to change the terms of the increasingly sterile debate over the case for public cultural subsidy. Since the 1980s the justification for funding arts and heritage has been framed, first in terms of the economic benefits that it brought through employment, regeneration and tourism, and then in terms of social benefits such as education, social harmony and the reduction of crime. These so-called instrumental arguments, which introduced a regime of targets and supposedly measurable outcomes, were in conflict with the argument that culture should be supported for its own sake, that its intrinsic qualities and merits were justification in themselves. Holden argued that neither instrumental values nor intrinsic values were mutually exclusive: rather, they had a positive and dynamic relationship, and that it was possible to devise a methodology that would articulate the value of culture in a more comprehensive and nuanced way than through the crude metrics of instrumental value, or hard-to-quantify assertions based on the idea that art is good of and for itself. Holden went further, and argued that there was a third form of value, produced by the actions of a cultural organisation in relation to its mission and its publics. This third form

Figure 1 Value triangle

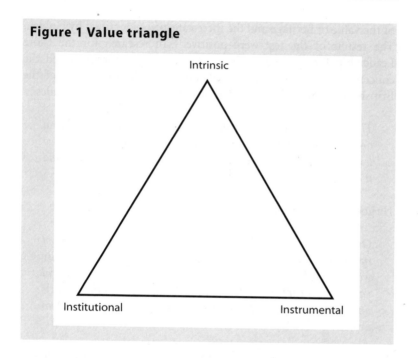

of value he called institutional value, and this is the primary focus of this essay.

Holden made it clear that instrumental, intrinsic and institutional value are different ways of looking at the same thing, but for the sake of simplicity expressed the three elements that combine as Cultural Value in the shape of an equilateral triangle.

Subsequent to the publication of *Capturing Cultural Value*, and an associated study, *Challenge and Change: HLF and Cultural Value*,[12] two independent studies have tested the practical application of this conceptual model. The Heritage Lottery Fund commissioned Opinion Leader Research to conduct two "Citizens' Juries" to test the Demos model with groups of people with no specific interest in heritage, and see if there was a correlation between their appreciation of the value of heritage and the three categories identified by Holden. The results of the test were positive.[13] In research for the Clore Leadership Programme a Clore Fellow, Stephen Escritt, tested the concept of Cultural Value in the context of the operations of the British Museum, and again found positive results. Escritt concludes:

> The process of applying the theory of cultural value to a cultural organisation has revealed that cultural value can work on two levels. It can work as a tool for organisational development and it can provide a better rationale for investment in culture.[14]

He goes on to argue:

> On an organisational level, cultural value can give a picture of the success – or failure – of the organisation in its own terms. By working backwards from a series of specific values, the cultural value model captures intrinsic value – the Holy Grail that arts and cultural organisations have always found so difficult to express.[15]

Although deploying different terms, Escritt's paper independently applies some the principles that will be proposed here.

Holden's follow-up essay, *Cultural Value and the Crisis of Legitimacy*, proposes that in the cultural sector a second triangular relationship is also in play. This is between the Politicians and policy-makers, who set cultural policy and provide the funds, the Professionals who use those funds to pursue their cultural objectives, (which might or might not conform to the Politicians' intentions), and the Public, who enjoy – or decline to participate in – the results.

While being careful to say that each group has interests in common, and that each will have at least some interest in each of the three sectors, Holden argues that the Politicians have a primary interest in Instrumental Value, the Public a primary interest in Intrinsic Value while being also interested in the benefits derived from Institutional Value, and that the Professionals, individually motivated

Figure 2 Relationship triangle

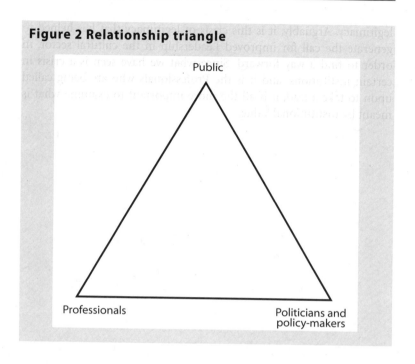

Public

Professionals

Politicians and
policy-makers

by Intrinsic Value, also have a concern for the Institutional Value created by the organisations in which they work.

Holden's point is that this triangular relationship has become distorted because none of the parties in the relationship entirely understands or appreciates the values of the other. Politicians encounter resistance to their instrumental policy goals, the Professionals feel frustrated at the failure of the Politicians to appreciate the intrinsic value of what they do, and the Public feel excluded from the argument between the Professionals and the Politicians. The Professionals fall back on their expertise and fail to produce the sort of institutional value that the Public wants. With all three parties dissatisfied with present arrangements, and lacking a common viewpoint, and a common language in which to discuss them, the system for public funding of culture faces a crisis of legitimacy. Arguably, it is this crisis of legitimacy that has helped to generate the call for improved Leadership in the cultural sector, in order to find a way forward. Since what we have seen is a crisis in certain institutions, and it is the Professionals who are being called upon to take a lead, it is all the more important to examine what is meant by Institutional Value.

5. Institutional Value and the Cultural Sector

While it is the case that all institutions have the capacity to have both positive and negative effects beyond their immediate activity – a widget factory may contribute to local prosperity but at the same time pollute the local environment – the question of what constitutes Institutional Value is especially important in the cultural sector because many of the benefits derived from cultural activity are intangible, and results are much harder to monetise than in the business world. This is not to suggest that commercial products do not have cultural, symbolic and aesthetic qualities. The emotions that influence consumer choice, and make one brand so much more powerful than another are also intangible, but these qualities and emotions are monetised through exchange value. A landscape, an old master in a public gallery, a sculpture in a park, or even a subsidised performance in a theatre or concert hall has a value that is not completely realised through price.

The theory of Institutional Value is partly derived from the work of Professor Mark H. Moore, of the Kennedy School of Government at Harvard University. In 1995 he published *Creating Public Value: Strategic Management in Government,* in which he addressed the question of what kind of value is produced by the managers of public services, as opposed to those of commercial enterprises. His answer was Public Value, the successful creation of which he defined as "initiating and reshaping public sector enterprises in ways that increase their value to the public in both the short and the long term".[16] Moore did not offer an elaborated definition of this key term. His approach, rather, was to demonstrate its creation in practice, through case studies taken from the American public sector.

In addition to introducing the concept of Public Value, Moore laid especial emphasis on the need for public sector managers to recognise that, far more than in the commercial sector, their operational context – what he calls their "authorizing" environment[17] – is political. This may be a reflection of the fact that local democracy is far less moribund in America than it is in Britain, but it is also the case that in Britain the tradition of the "arm's length principle" (discussed below) has obscured the power relations that exist both at national and local authority level. Since the creation of a full-blooded "Ministry of Culture", first as the Department of National Heritage in 1992, and then the Department for Culture, Media and Sport in 1997 the political context in the United Kingdom has become more explicit. Devolution in Scotland and Wales in particular has produced tensions between the Politicians and the Professionals over the direction and "ownership" of cultural policy.

Moore's concept of Public Value was taken up and refined in a discussion paper released by the Cabinet Office Strategy Unit in 2002. From the authors' perspective, Public Value is something produced by government through laws, regulation, services and other actions, and is distinguished by being something for which the public must be willing to give something up in exchange, either through taxation, restriction on their individual rights of action (such as in planning), or through voluntary participation. The public wants efficient public services, but also things less easily quantified such as social justice, equitable distribution and proper stewardship of the public realm. They also want to feel engaged with the public realm, and public services that are responsive to their views.

With the satisfaction of basic needs, the public has become concerned not just about the quantity of service provision, but also the quality. This moves the debate on from arguments about instrumental outcomes into the ethics, and even aesthetics, of public service delivery:

> *There is . . . evidence that the ethos and culture of an organisation is very important in determining the extent to which services create/destroy value. An extensive management literature offers different models for understanding these cultural variables in performance: one commonly used distinction is between culture (fundamental attitudes and belief systems), climate (explicit behavioural characteristics, e.g how managers treat staff) and values (taking an individual rather than organisational perspective on priorities and motivations of staff). All these aspects are linked, and can affect the performance of a public service organisation and its ability to create value.*[18]

The concept of Public Value has been found to be particularly useful in addressing issues of ethics and social behaviour that governments find especially difficult directly to influence, most importantly the question of the public's trust in the institutions that serve them. The Strategy Unit document argues: "Public value encourages managers to think of goals, such as maintaining legitimacy, that go beyond organisational survival and meeting immediate service delivery targets".[19] It also means that attention has to be given to the process by which services are delivered, as well as to the quantifiable outcomes that are the focus of the practices of the New Public Management adopted by government in the 1980s.

One organisation that has seized on the possibilities offered by the theory of Public Value is the BBC, a public service broadcaster with an international as well as national role that is also a powerful commercial player, but which is dependent for its survival on a hypothecated poll tax, the annual license fee. It is also draws its legitimacy – in the narrow legal sense – from the periodic renewal of its Royal Charter, which sets the terms and limits of its operational context. The renewal of the Royal Charter is a highly sensitive political issue, and in June 2004, in preparation for the next renewal, the BBC published *Building Public Value*, which made its case in the new language of Public Value:

> Because the BBC is a public organisation, it is able to make a unique contribution to the UK's broadcasting system. While commercial broadcasters aim to create shareholder value, the BBC exists solely to create public value. The BBC creates public value by serving people both as individuals and as citizens. For people as individuals, the BBC aims to provide a range of programmes that inform, educate and entertain, that people enjoy and value for what they are. For people in their role as citizens, the BBC seeks to offer additional benefits over and above individual value. It aims to contribute to the wider well-being of society, through its contribution to the UK's democracy, culture and quality of life.[20]

The document went on ingeniously to argue that the Public Value created by the BBC was also an economic value:

> The BBC is capable of creating substantial positive economic value, for example through its stimulation of the UK's creative economy. Of course, parts of the BBC's economic impact can be negative – for example, where it may reduce audiences for a rival commercial service. The economic value of the BBC therefore needs to be a net calculation. The sum total of the BBC's individual value, citizen value and economic value is the public value of the BBC – a measure of its contribution to the quality of life in the UK .[21]

Thus the BBC used the theory of Public Value to separate out the two political challenges that it faced: the terms on which its charter should be renewed, or in other words how wide its remit should be, an issue that has profound commercial implications for broadcasting as a whole, and the narrower question of what the future level of the license fee should be. The BBC has been successful in the first instance, although it has had to accept changes to its form of governance. At the time of writing the matter of the license fee, which will determine the BBC's capacity to carry out its public service mission, has yet to be settled.

The BBC is the first British organisation to make a persuasive link between Public Value and culture, but none of the documents that have been cited here uses the term Institutional Value. Neither Moore's *Creating Public Value* nor the Cabinet Strategy Unit refers to the arts, although Moore uses a public library as an example, and he has subsequently published a study of the operations of the arts agencies sponsored by individual American states, *Creating Public Value Through State Arts Agencies* (2005).[22] Holden's use of the term Cultural Value distinguishes it from the general category, Public Value, because it specifically describes the synthesis of values that are generated in the cultural sector: intrinsic, instrumental and institutional. As has been argued, Intrinsic Value will be most often experienced at an individual level, and Instrumental Value impacts most clearly on the collective. Institutional Value, however, is experienced both at the individual level and by society as a whole.

Institutional Value is created (or destroyed) by the interaction between an institution and its stakeholders, including the public at large. Very schematically, this interaction can be expressed in terms of three different kinds of relationship:

- O Engagement
- O Service
- O Trust

Engagement

Engagement describes the interaction between a cultural organisation and its audience when it mounts a performance, stages an exhibition, issues a publication or in some other way performs its function as a cultural institution. As the word suggests, this is a two-way process, initiated by the institution but one that has to be responsive to the needs and opinions of the intended audience. It goes without saying that to produce the maximum Institutional Value this engagement has to be judged successful, both by the organisation and its public. This will depend not only on the competence of the institution and its willingness to respond, but the creativity it brings to the engagement, as will be discussed later.

Service

Cultural organisations relate to their stakeholders and their audiences in ways that extend beyond performance. Consumer surveys show that how people are treated by the staff they encounter is rated only just behind the price and quality of what is being provided. Clear information is essential, and Institutional Value will be enhanced when the public has a sense that it is being offered a choice from a range of possibilities. The greater the mutual exchange, even "co-production" between audience and organisation the better. Organisations have to provide their stakeholders with information, and communicate with their audience through marketing. The price they set on their activities is in itself a form of communication, and the box office and information desk are key tools in their communication strategies. Service in terms of atmosphere, security, cleanliness and catering all add to Institutional Value. More profoundly, it is essential that the organisation presents itself as being at the service of the interests of its public, and that its own "producer interest" does not damage that relationship. The perceived arrogance of a cultural organisation can destroy Institutional Value.

Trust

Productive engagement and good service will generate a sense of trust between an organisation and its stakeholders, and will generate loyalty from its publics. Although this is the hardest relationship to quantify, it is the most important of all. Trust is a form of social capital, it creates a sense of identification between the organisation and those to whom it relates, which can be expressed as a feeling of "ownership" on the part of the public. An institution can do more than contribute to local or national pride; it can become symbolic of a collective identity and a local distinctiveness. Loss of trust, when people feel that they have been let down, exploited, patronised or treated unfairly has profoundly negative effects on Institutional Value.

6. Loss of Trust: a case history

Trust is such an important yet hard to define concept, that it can be easier to recognise through its absence that its presence. It is ironic that an example of the damage that occurs to an organisation when there is a breakdown in trust is provided by one of the organisations commissioned by the Chancellor to deliver the national Cultural Leadership Programme.

In July 2005, having in recent years been "upsized, downsized, outsourced and restructured",[23] Arts Council England was subjected to a "Peer Review", a rapid, but high level and highly focussed interrogation by outside experts that is intended to give the Department for Culture, Media and Sport a greater insight into an organisation's successes and failures than that provided by the meeting of targets under Funding Agreements. The team of what might called friendly critics discovered that ACE had suffered a loss of trust, both with the arts community and its sponsoring body, the DCMS. Their key recommendation was: "Arts Council England and DCMS must work together to rebuild mutual trust, and to cement working relationships at the both the strategic and operational levels".[24] The short term effect of this breakdown in trust was failures of communication between ACE and its sponsoring ministry, and an even greater loss of trust brought by the decision of the DCMS to appoint its own art form officers in parallel to those of ACE.

The loss of trust between ACE and the sector that it is supposed to both lead and serve is equally serious. The dissolution, in the interests of "efficiency", of the former unpaid advisory art form panels, which created a form of permanent peer review at a lower level, has led to a disconnection between ACE's national office and the arts constituency. At the same time, there was a lack of confidence in the expertise of ACE's staff. The peer review expressed "concerns about Arts Council England's credibility within the arts community, and in particular about the ability of its officers to speak authoritatively on individual art forms".[25] The apparent weakness at officer level was compounded by confusion about the role and composition of ACE's governing body, the Council: "There seemed to be uncertainty about both what it does and how it does it".[26]

Steps have been taken to remedy this situation, but the ACE Peer Review provides more than a particular case study in the loss of institutional trust, because it goes to the heart of the problem facing the cultural sector: the crisis of legitimacy. Traditionally, relations between Politicians and Professionals in the cultural sector have been governed by the arms' length principle. Technically, this is a legal term for a relationship between two parties in which neither has control or advantage over the other, but in his report for the Gulbenkian Foundation in 1976, *Support for the Arts in England and Wales*, the judge Lord Redcliffe-Maud applied it to the relationship between government and the Arts Council.

> *By self-denying ordinance the politicians leave the Council free to spend as it thinks fit. No minister needs to reply to questions in Parliament about the beneficiaries – or about unsuccessful applicants for an Arts Council grant. A convention has been established over the years that in arts patronage neither the politician nor the bureaucrat knows best.*[27]

It is tempting to be cynical about the reality of the arms' length principle, for such are the common interests of Britain's ruling cultural class, and such is the method of their selection, Council members can usually be relied on to do the politicians' bidding without having to be told. This was certainly the view of the cultural critic Raymond Williams, who served on the Council in the 1970s: "The true social process of such bodies as the Arts Council is one of administered consensus by co-option".[28] But the key to the arms' length principle is trust, and as Michael Power argues in *The Audit Society* (1997)[29] the practices of the New Public Management that were developed in the 1980s and 1990s have, in the interests of greater accountability and government control, destroyed trust. Over-regulated by the imposition of targets through its Funding Agreement, and evidently under-esteemed by the DCMS, it is no wonder that there has been a crisis of confidence in, and at, Arts Council England. ACE is embarking on its own "Public Value Inquiry", with a widespread public consultation.[30]

7. The Institutional Value Triangle

Engagement, service and trust are mutually supporting aspects of the relationship between a cultural organisation, its stakeholders and its publics. To produce the maximum Institutional Value, an organisation should conceptualise its approach to this relationship under three, also mutually supporting, headings.

To express this diagrammatically, what is needed is a new conceptual triangle.

Creativity

None of the other benefits attributed to cultural activity can be achieved if the primary *creative* purpose is not achieved – even though these purposes will vary. Different institutions will have different forms of engagement. As Adrian Ellis has written:

> It is, for example, the goal of some arts organisations to support and develop a given canon of work, and to act as stewards of that tradition; it is the goal of others to provide opportunities for individual development through the transformational experiences that culture can provide; and others to provide and build expressive and emotional bonds through communal participation.[31]

The aims of a great symphony orchestra will be different from those a

Figure 3 Institutional Value triangle

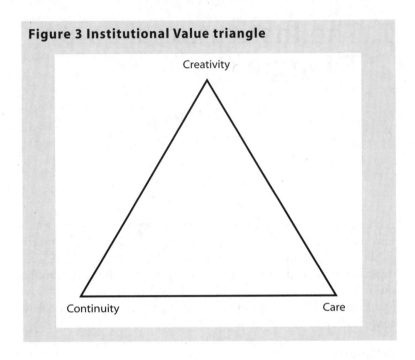

community theatre seeking to raise local consciousness about the environment, but it is the way they set about these goals that is of primary significance. A poor production will not change hearts and minds any more than a poor performance will enhance the reputation of classical music. But as the doyen of opera producers, Sir Peter Jonas has argued, whatever the chosen form, the emphasis must be not on "representation" of the work, but "interpretation", for it is in the interpretation that creativity is to be found.[32]

"Creativity", like Trust, is an elusive concept. It is a primary purpose of all cultural institutions, and it is this that Gordon Brown wants to capture – but it can be argued that in one sense a great many cultural institutions are not creative at all. Of course, they offer creative interpretations of the cultural canon, and add to it with new work, but they operate in what might be called a "mature market", with a fixed conception of the audience that they are trying to reach, and a conventional and well-established way of delivering their work. The National Theatre is an admirable institution that presents excellent productions, but it is also pinned down by the building that it occupies and the cultural conventions it was set up to serve. By contrast, the organisation Artangel has no fixed performance or gallery space, is not committed to any particular cultural medium – it has commissioned works involving theatre, film, music, sculpture, radio – and shows little interest in producing works that are permanent. Similarly, it relates to its audience through finding unconventional locations and public spaces in which to present its commissions.[33]

Like is not being compared with like here, which is precisely the point. It is possible that in time Artangel will become as conventional and established in its own terms as the National Theatre, as it follows the familiar trajectory from the *avant-garde* to the academy, from leading the way with the development of new forms of expression and new ways of seeing the world, to becoming devoted to the conservation of a body of work and the policing of "standards". The academy has its uses as a form of collective memory, as an archive of repertoire and practice, but it is not a crucible for innovation, and those entrusted with a memorial function – which can be orchestras or theatres as much as museums – need to find new ways of connecting the heritage aspect of their work with contemporary conditions. This can be achieved in surprising ways: the "authentic practices" movement in orchestral music was a stimulating challenge to increasingly ossified ways of presenting the repertoire.

In order to be truly creative, cultural organisations need to avoid the process by which entrepreneurship is gradually supplanted by bureaucracy. They begin by looking forwards and outwards towards future goals, finding new ways to achieve them. But as they become established they start to look inwards, and end up looking backwards, and therefore are resistant to change. Organisations must always look forwards, since decisions about policy will always be about the future, not the past.

They therefore need to think creatively not only about the work they do but also the way that they organise themselves. The standard organisational form of a British cultural organisation is that of a charity limited by guarantee. This has certain tax advantages, and although it is not obligatory to be a charity to receive public funding, the funding system finds this the most convenient constitutional form for the receipt of public money. A charity is not precluded from making a profit on its operations, provided the profit is applied solely to the stated purposes of the charity, but too often the "not-for-profit" concept means "expecting-to-make-a-loss". The price of bridging the gap between income and expenditure is submission to the regulation and policy directions of an external funding body whose understanding of the arms' length principle may not be as liberal as that of the charity. A degree of initiative, independence and self-reliance will be surrendered, however benign the intentions of the funder. As has already been pointed out, members of the board of a charity are legally precluded from having a direct financial interest in the success of the organisation, which may inhibit the creative and entrepreneurial spirit. Good governance is not necessarily guaranteed by leaving the fate of most cultural organisations in the hands of unpaid volunteers with very variable skills and sometimes-conflicting motives.

A simplified charitable model is coming on stream in the form of the Charitable Incorporated Organisation, which only has to report to the Charity Commission, and not, as in the case of traditional charities, to Companies House as well, but it will take time to see if this form proves viable. Alternative, and possibly more entre-preneurial, models do exist. The music producing, presenting and publishing company Serious, with its interest in jazz, world and contemporary music, bridges the commercial and not-for-profit spheres it inhabits by operating principally as Serous Ltd, a company limited by shares, with paid directors, which takes the commercial risks. But it also has two subsidiary not-for-profit companies limited by guarantee that undertake projects that need to attract public and other third party funding. (A not-for-profit company does not have shares and does not distribute profits to its members, which are retained for the benefit of the company. It has directors rather than trustees.) The company's members have to guarantee a limited sum for any liabilities in the event of liquidation.

The directors of Serious chose not to have a board of trustees, as would be required by having charity status, because they felt that this mode of governance could not respond quickly enough to the sort of rapid decision making their activities called for. The combined accounts of the Serious group of enterprises show a turnover of £3.5 million a year, and an operating profit. According to a case study by AEA Consulting: "The commercial arm helps facilitate partnerships with the music business, which takes an uncomprehending view of the not-for-profit sector, while the subsidiary companies are assisting Serious to become an attractive proposition for funding bodies". [34]

A second possible model is the Community Interest Company, a new form of company that became a legal option in 2005. The Community Interest Company was devised in order to encourage enterprise for the public good by creating a form of company that can be at the service of organisations that trade to further a social cause. These causes, and the extent of their commercial activity, may restrict their ability to become charities, but this model allows them to use commercial means to achieve social ends.

Such a company can be established as limited by shares or by guarantee, as a private company or a public limited company, but it has to be registered with the relevant Regulator, who has to be satisfied that its activities will be of public benefit. Once registered, a Community Interest Company must file an annual report showing that that is indeed the case, and that an "asset lock" is in place to guarantee that purely private interests are not being served. A Community Interest Company can pay its directors, and companies that chose to issue shares are allowed to issue capped dividends to investors, which is intended to encourage both philanthropic and commercial investment. Community Interest Companies can also apply for National Lottery funds. The emphasis on "community" and community purposes might limit the ability of a more general cultural organisation to qualify for registration as such a company, but of the more than four hundred companies registered to date, a number of community theatres and others arts organisations have been registered. Since the creation of public benefit is one of the measures of Cultural Value, the Cultural Value argument could well be deployed in justification of an application for registration as a Community Interest Company.

Funding bodies, as well as the organisations they fund, need to be more creative about their structures. The ruling model is bureaucratic: the Department for Culture, Media and Sport funds some institutions directly, such as those belonging to the National Museum Directors' Conference (which includes the British Library and the National Archives) but passes on the bulk of its funding to be distributed by NDPBs (non-departmental public bodies) such as Arts Council England and the Museum, Libraries and Archives Council, which constitute a second tier, arms' length bureaucracy. The present system is more than sixty years old, and has become sclerotic through the perpetuation of historic funding. While there are very few commercial companies that are more than fifty years old, it seems politically impossible to close down moribund cultural organisations, thus limiting the space for the creation of new ones. Funding bodies tend to deal only with the known, are hierarchical and centripetal in structure and have a bureaucratic tendency to favour routine and established practice. As bureaucracies, they look for reflections of themselves in the organisations they fund. None of this is conducive to creativity, which relies on crossing established boundaries, breaking routines and thinking outside the bureaucratic box.

Again, alternative models do exist. The nine Regional Screen Agencies in England were set up between 2001 and 2003 to promote both the culture and the economy of film and the moving image in all its aspects, through encouraging production, exhibition, training, education and archiving. There is no central bureaucracy, and while they receive core funding from the DCMS via the United Kingdom Film Council, they have funding partnerships with the Regional Development Agencies, the Sector Skills Council for the audio-visual industries, the European Regional Development Fund, the European Social Fund, the National Lottery, Arts Council England, local government and other public funding. They respond to the policy interests of not just the DCMS but also the Department for Education and Science, the Department for Trade and Industry, the Department for Communities and Local Government, and the Foreign and Commonwealth Office. This need for collaboration and partnership on the input side of the Regional Screen Agencies is reflected on the output side, where, with staffs averaging no more than 15, the RSAs see themselves not as funders, but as brokers and investors, using their knowledge to find partnership funding for projects and their own funds as catalytic investments. This devolved, mobile and inventive "agency model" for public funding, which avoids creating a dependency-relationship between the agent and its partners, has much to recommend it.[35]

Public purposes change, and public institutions must be prepared to change with them. That does not mean that there has to be organisational change for its own sake, but when it becomes clear that it is necessary, it has to be driven from within the organisation, not from outside it. "Change" has its downside if it is externally imposed, as has been the case with Arts Council England, where it weakens trust, as we have seen. The Museums, Libraries and Archives Council is on its third reorganisation since its creation in 2000.

Continuity

For an organisation to remain creative, it must embrace change. Yet – and this conveys the dynamic of the Cultural Value triangle, which acknowledges the tension between its three aspects and allows for different viewpoints at different times – cultural organisations, while delivering constant change in what they make, also have to deliver consistency of quality. An artist's reputation is not built on one canvas, or a gallery's on one exhibition. It is in this context that precisely those bureaucratic procedures that can stifle creativity turn out to be needed to underpin it. Order, reliability, and above all financial responsibility are an essential part of Institutional Value. A balance sheet may only be a snapshot of the past, but no organisation can rationally plan for the future without knowing where it has come from. In particular, cultural organisations need to pay greater attention to the information that it can gain from its publics.

A report commissioned by the Arts Councils of England, Scotland and Wales in 2003 concluded:

> *There is a clear lack of a business planning culture within most arts organisations which manifests itself in a lack of demand for audience data which could otherwise have been needed to inform planning. Conversely, those managers who are keen to have information about audiences often find it difficult to access what they need.*[36]

Where audience information is gathered, it tends to be used for marketing purposes only, and "a strong need was identified in the consultation for audience data to be used as a management tool as well as a marketing tool".[37] It is possible to have some sympathy with the apparent data-phobia of cultural organisations when one reads that "many organisations find it extremely vexing to have to present the same information in subtly different ways to different funders (and sometimes to different departments of the same funding body)".[38] This comment reflects a wider problem with the way cultural organisations set about evaluating themselves in order to provide continuity of service and plan for the future.

As Sara Selwood has shown in her article "The Politics of Data Collection", reams of data have been generated in the last two decades about the impact of the arts and culture on the British economy and society. But the drive to gather this information has been from the top down, rather than the bottom up. The political demand for ever greater accountability created by the New Public Management and reflected in the growth of the Audit Society has generated an accountancy ladder that descends from the Treasury to government spending departments to the Non Departmental Public Bodies and local authorities to the organisations that these fund. Suitably prepared gobbets of information are then fed back up the food chain, sometimes, as we have seen, "the same information in subtly different ways". Rightly, accounting for public money is a political obligation, but government policies shift over time, so that the information has to be recast (or different information found) to fit the political agenda of the moment. The effect of this is twofold: little data has any longitudinal use, as the boxes to be filled keep changing, and the purpose of the data gathered is to show that often moving targets are being met, rather than to generate useful knowledge about the organisation.

There are also severe doubts about the ability of the methodologies that have been used in the past to demonstrate economic and social impact to capture the totality of the contribution of culture to the public realm – which is why the concept of Cultural Value has been developed. Writing of recent reviews of the evidence of the social impact of cultural projects, Selwood states:

> *The consensus is that much of the evidence presented is invalid –*
> *although the reasons cited for this differ. They include the non-*
> *substantiation of claims; the antagonism of cultural institutions*
> *towards the collection and use of data; the fact that projects have*
> *limited jurisdiction and limited potential to influence outcomes;*
> *the lack of robustness of the methodologies used; the quality of*
> *evidence gathered; and a failure of reporting methods.*[39]

Such doubts about the evidence have not prevented reports and impact surveys being produced in large numbers, especially around the time of government Comprehensive Spending Reviews, but the purpose of the evidence gathered, whether such evidence is valid or not, is not to inform policy, but to influence it through advocacy. The "good stories" get told, the bad ones glossed over.

The foregoing is not an argument against accountability or the need for evidence. Self-evaluation is part of the creative process: the evaluations conducted by cultural organisations should not be externally imposed, but generated by the needs of the organisation, and set in terms that are useful to the organisation as well as any external funder. Above all, data needs to be gathered consistently over time, so that a body of knowledge is created, not loose bundles of information contingent on short-term expediency and shifting political agendas.

The need for continuity reflects the service aspect of an organisation's relationship with its stakeholders. It has to be consistent in its dealings with its funders, with the people whose work it presents and with those who supply it with the means and materials it needs to do its work. It must give a reliable standard of service to its audience. This is more easily achieved if the organisation shows that it is able to learn from experience, that it values the experience of those who work in it, and that it has a secure sense of its own place and purpose: in other words, a story about itself that secures its identity across time. It is remarkable how few organisations are aware of their history, even in the short term. The aim of any organisation must be its own sustainability, which calls for sound management, investment in training and a prudent approach to risk. This does not contradict the need for a cultural organisation to constantly recreate itself, for this too is part of the continuity of the organisation as it develops and grows.

Care

The principle that an organisation must show due care might be thought to be no more than it should be aware of current legislation on health and safety, and avoid waste. But true care is shown when an organisation thinks of its dealings with its public and stakeholders in terms of a relationship, not a transaction. That does not preclude the organisation from showing leadership by shaping that relationship by communicating its values and informing public taste. Public value may be tautologically defined as what the public values, but as Ricardo Blaug has argued in a recent presentation on behalf of the Work Foundation, it is not just a question of an organisation being responsive to perceived public desires, but of entering into a creative relationship with the public. There needs to be a virtuous educational circle: the organisation learns from its public, and its public learns from the organisation.

This process of generating "refined preferences" demands genuine public consultation and user participation on the one hand, and good communications and educational initiatives on the other. Blaug argues that this process of refining preferences:

> *Is not a way of re-asserting the refined, high-end tastes of the middle or upper classes. But it does require some thought to have taken place among the public. It means that something took place beyond a mere reactive jolt, that some consideration or discussion went into a decision that was made in the public's name and with it's money. A preference is more influential if it is well informed, educated, negotiated, discussed, chewed-over and then given. The public might still hold the same views, but the fact that these were arrived at via a defensible process significantly increases the public's demand to be heard. To an economist, this is about addressing an asymmetry of information. But it is also more than this, for it gives a democratic justification for why the public needs to better understand what the public purse provides on its behalf.*[40]

The process described here is one answer to the "crisis of legitimacy" that has undermined the confidence of the cultural sector.

By providing high quality work and good service, an institution will build up a relationship with its publics (and stakeholders) that will generate loyalty and trust. Confidence in the efficacy and efficiency of cultural organisations contributes to the creation of social capital through the two-way relationship described above. Formal and informal trust is generated through an organisation's good governance, the quality of its decision-taking, and the transparency of its operations. Only the largest cultural organisations produce annual reports, and these are hardly more informative than those of limited companies. The difference is that publicly quoted commercial companies hold shareholder's meetings, at which it is, at least in theory, possible to question the directors. As far as is known, no publicly funded cultural organisation has held a stakeholders' meeting on similar lines.

The principles of care have to be applied internally as well as externally. As Richard Sennett argues: "Loyalty is a participatory relationship; no business plan alone, beautiful or logical as it may be, will earn the loyalty of those on whom it is imposed, simply because the employees have not participated in its gestation".[41] And as Sennett goes on to point out, employee loyalty will help organisations survive the downturn of a business cycle. In the cultural sector, organisations have to cope with the vicissitudes of the funding cycle, as governments trim their expenditure, prisoners themselves of the electoral and business cycle.

Externally, the need for the alignment of the public's values with those of the organisation through public involvement has already been referred to, but once the alignment has been achieved to create a sense of common culture, other aspects of Cultural Value that are expressive of care can be brought more effectively into play. If the principle of encouraging and widening access is clearly communicated, the public will accept that policies will be targeted at specific groups or specific areas of the country. Similarly, while people agree that the overall benefit of cultural subsidy should be universally available, the principle of equity and fairness will not be seen to conflict with policies that try to ensure that the benefits of subsidy should go most to those most in need. With trust securely in place, people will more willingly accept policies that promote diversity and equal opportunities. In the long-term, they will accept the notion of inter-generational equity that is the foundation of true heritage: the present generation is only the steward of the historic environment, and has a duty to pass it on to future generations in as un-degraded a condition as possible.

Corporate Responsibility is a watchword in commercial organisations, but how much more important is this is when the organisation depends on public subsidy for its existence. Beyond the regenerative effects that cultural organisations can have, their environmental impact appears to be an unexplored aspect of their activities. Heritage organisations, in particular, can argue that the conservation and re-use of existing buildings make a positive contribution, since the re-use of a building consumes 27% less energy than new construction, and creates less waste and consequent landfill.[42] Conserved landscape and woodlands create "carbon sinks", and although the results are unpredictable, every cultural organisation should conduct an energy and carbon emission audit.

The principle of Care and the practice of Service are not a threat to the professionalism of those working in a cultural organisation. Their ability to show care and to deliver service depends on their creative, managerial and financial expertise. In return, the legitimacy of their expertise is reinforced by the positive response from their publics. But the relationship depends on a more democratic approach: as Holden has argued: "cultural professionals need to engage more, and differently, with the public in order to merit a broad-based democratic mandate".[43] Since funding decisions, such as that to launch a national Cultural Leadership Programme are political, the democratic political process has an entirely legitimate role to play. The challenge to the professionals is actively to engage with it.

8. Evaluating Institutional Value

Having done so much in our earlier work to challenge methodologies of measurement and the regime of targets, tables and testing, it may seem counter-intuitive to raise the question of how the success or otherwise of the *application* of this tool can be measured. But the analytical categories that have been suggested here form the basis for evaluating the outcomes of the process. It assumes that the organisation will assess its overall mission and purpose in terms of Cultural Value, and then seek to define what values it creates as an institution.

Very importantly, the adoption of Institutional Value as an analytical tool is in itself part of the process of creating Institutional Value, and the identification of the appropriate categories by and for each particular organisation is the beginning of the Institutional Value process. It will be appreciated that the three elements of Cultural Value interlock, so that it is possible to argue, as does Escritt, for instance, in his testing of the principle as applied to the British Museum, that education is so central to the ethos of that particular institution that learning outcomes are expressive of Intrinsic rather than Instrumental Value.[44] In the case of Institutional Value, Creativity, Continuity and Care are mutually supporting practices whose expression may well emerge in overlapping forms. Thus an organisation's contribution to the Quality of Life Indicators used by national and local government might be included in all three segments, but positive Quality of Life indicators certainly should be considered as contributing both to the continuity and longevity of the organisation, and as an index of the care shown. Audience surveys, media and peer reviews will produce both quantitative and qualitative assessments.

Below is a schematic suggestion of discrete areas to be evaluated, in order to arrive at a total picture. Some outcomes can be rendered in figures, but others will need more complex forms of assessment. The application of the whole process is in itself an indicator of the transparency of the organisation.

It will have been noticed that several sources of evaluative information, and several means of evaluation appear in relation to more than one field of practice. That is deliberate, because the three areas of practice are not mutually exclusive, but mutually reinforcing. To change the metaphorical geometry for a moment, Creativity, Continuity and Care form a benign circle, where Care can lead to Creativity, and Continuity support Care.

Figure 4 The Institutional Value matrix

PRACTICE	SOCIAL DIVIDEND	EVALUATION
CREATIVITY	Engagement with Stakeholders Core activity of organisation Opportunity for audience participation and self-expression	Mission statement Cultural programme Audience figures Media review Peer review Artistic risk review Publications Intellectual Property created Learning outcomes Partnerships Self-assessment Awards gained Economic contribution

Figure 4 *continued*

PRACTICE	SOCIAL DIVIDEND	EVALUATION
CONTINUITY	Service to stakeholders Health of organisation Engagement from staff	Governance Strategic plan Information management, especially longitudinal data Audience figures Media review Peer review Funder relationships: spread of funding base Financial position Value for Money Intellectual Property exploited Staff turnover Staff training Volunteer engagement Friends' organisation Subscription scheme Contribution to Quality of Life Contribution to local distinctiveness Brand value
CARE	Growth of social capital: trust from stakeholders, loyalty from staff and audience, positive responses to the organisation	Audience surveys Media review Peer review Focus groups Citizens' juries Education programme Volunteers Friends' organisation "co-production" with audience Contribution to Quality of Life Donations Health & Safety record Environmental impact

These general concepts offer a framework within which more precise categories of activity, directly applicable to the institution in question, can be developed. To go back to the difference between a symphony orchestra and a community theatre, the principles apply to both, but they will have evidence and outcomes that are appropriately different to the organisation. While there is a case for establishing cross-sectoral comparability when it comes to audience and financial data, a one-size-fits-all approach to Institutional Value is a contradiction of the diversity that helps to generate the creativity of the sector. It is for this reason that the organisation itself – and all those working in the organisation – must evolve its own specific categories, and sets its own benchmarks. They will be there to help the organisation do its work, not hinder it, and enable the organisation to recognise its true purposes and what it does best.

9 The Role of Leadership

Institutional Value is a conceptual framework that offers a critical tool to be used by an organisation to examine its current practices, and remodel them if necessary. The process will involve examining its organisational capacity, its creative drive, its ethical stance, even its environmental responsibility. The creative process of self-evaluation is very likely to produce internal change and possibly a shift in direction. Certainly it will generate a renewed sense of purpose. Internal change is likely to lead to a change in external relationships. An organisation that sets out to identify its own goals and define for itself its contribution to the public realm will not need to have them imposed by external funders. Just as its relationship with its publics is defined as a service rather than a transaction, the nature of its accountability to its funders will be defined by partnership and respect, not grudging form filling.

Although the concept of Institutional Value has not hitherto been explicitly applied, there are examples of the sort of organisational self-refurbishment being carried out along the lines proposed. In 2002 Parks Canada, which is responsible for a group of National Parks, National Historic Sites and other heritage and environmental assets covering 3% of the Canadian land mass, adopted a new charter setting out the values and principles governing the provision of its services. To achieve this Parks Canada created a union-management team that involved more than 5,000 employees in two rounds of consultation:

> A consensus view settled on three human-resource-management principles: competence, fairness and respect. The external values were also subject to lengthy consultation. The final version of the charter, adopted in 2002, set out Parks Canada's role in deceptively simple language: guardians, guides, partners and storytellers. Despite that simplicity, the Parks Canada Charter captures in a formal way a significant shift in the way the institution carries out its work.[45]

Ultimately, however, it is not "institutions" that change things, it is the people within them. To adopt the principles of Institutional Value will require courage, and leadership. Mark Moore has argued that in recognising and applying the principles of Public Value: "the primary change being recommended is *in the thoughts and actions of managers*, not in the existing institutional arrangements that hold them accountable".[46] It is in this context that the emphasis of Leadership training on individuals, not organisations, and on behaviours, not skills, acquires a rationale.

It is therefore to the new Leaders that the critical tool of Institutional Value is offered, but, as has already been pointed out, it is essential that the process be owned by the whole organisation, that is to say, by every individual within it. The process must be one of internal self-realisation, not external audit. This will lead to improved motivation, which in turn will lead to improved performance. And if the relationship between leaders and the organisations they lead is reconceived in this way, both preferred models of leadership and models of organisations may change. Indeed, it is essential to the creativity and continuity of the organisation that they should.

In his latest study, *Leadership: Limits and Possibilities*, Keith Grint, Professor of Leadership Studies at Lancaster University argues: "In effect, leadership is the property and consequence of a community rather than the property and consequence of an individual leader". [47]

As a result, he goes on to make the case for a neglected aspect of Leadership theory, Followership:

> *In effect, power is a consequence as much as a cause of followership: if – and only if – followers follow leaders become powerful, but that act remains contingent not determined . . . followers always have the choice not to act, and though they may pay the consequences of not acting the point is that no leader or situation can guarantee followership – leaders are neither omnipotent nor omniscient – but irresponsible followers can make them appear both. Worse, irresponsible followers allow irresponsible leaders to take us to their private and unachievable utopias via three-easy-steps that usually include (1) blaming someone else for everything; (2) leaving all decisions in the hands of the leader and ceasing to take personal responsibility for actions taken in their name; and (3) taking on trust the leader's version of the 'truth'.*[48]

This is a challenge both to the leaders and the led. Followers must recognise their responsibilities and be prepared to challenge the leader with what Grint calls "Constructive Dissent".[49] Even more importantly, there is a challenge to the mode of "transformational", "charismatic", or "heroic" leadership that has been the prevailing style, especially in the cultural sector. As opposed to the "transactional" leader – basically a bureaucratic figure who will ensure the maintenance of procedures and the delivery of pre-set targets – the "transformational" leader is a visionary who can inspire his followers (the gender choice reflects current reality) and take an organisation to new places. In the decade or so when the National Lottery made possible a previously undreamed of number of building projects, this style may well have been needed, but there is a downside: charismatic leaders are liable to succumb to a dangerous narcissism that causes them to see reality only in terms of their own reflection, and leaders and their followers may suffer from the destabilisation and burn-out that can be the consequences of making the heroic efforts that are called for to transform an organisation.

There is, however, an alternative model of Leadership, "relational leadership". Such leaders inspire and motivate, and generate change, but are also concerned to communicate with their followers, to nurture their abilities, and to reward them by creating a collective ownership of the organisation's success. While being no less committed to Creativity, relational Leadership is more conducive to long-term stability, to Continuity and Care. Less demonstrative in style, so much so that it is sometimes referred to as "invisible" Leadership, relational Leadership can be seen as a more feminine style, irrespective of the leader's gender. Coupled with Grint's concept of Followership with its crucial element of "Constructive Dissent", and acknowledging that Leadership is needed at every level in an organisation, and not just at the top, we arrive at the concept of Distributed Leadership, neither a hierarchy nor anarchy, but a heterarchy, where power and responsibility is widely shared throughout the organisation, in a collective commitment to the principles of Creativity, Continuity and Care.

Above all, the principle of creating social capital through the generation and enhancement of Trust means that, in contrast to the audit culture of the New Public Management, leaders (and followers) in cultural organisations must be given a new mandate to manage themselves with creative freedom. By adopting the principles of Institutional Value they will earn a new legitimacy, become genuinely accountable to their stakeholders, and be re-empowered as Professionals. Mark Moore has warned that public managers see themselves as primarily servants of the political process, not principals within that service: "their orientation is *downward*, toward the reliable control of organisational operations rather than either *outward*, toward the achievement of valuable results, or *upward*, toward renegotiating policy mandates".[50] The adoption of Institutional Value as a critical tool is one means by which they can look upwards, and become more confidently active in the public realm.

10. Conclusion: What the cultural sector has to teach

If the cultural sector is not to remain a sideshow in the great affairs of state, it will require more than kinds words at 7.30 in the morning, welcome though they are. A commitment of as little as 0.5 per cent of government expenditure to investment in the sector would have a transformative effect, and enable the new leaders that will emerge from the Chancellor's national Cultural Leadership Programme to seize the opportunity offered.

The wisdom of Gordon Brown's words lay in the recognition of the ever-greater blurring of our public and commercial cultures. The publicly funded cultural sector has the potential to make a significant contribution to the economic well being of the country, as well as the capacity to address the complex moral and social issues that are created by the public "illth" that sits beside the creation of private wealth. Given renewed confidence, it can enhance and expand the capacity to create the ideas, images and values upon which a future economy will increasingly depend, and which business and industry will need to support.

What business can learn about Creativity is that the cultural sector lives in a world of one-offs, as opposed to the profitable repetitions of the assembly line. It is true that there are long running musicals, formulaic popular music and recyclable television formats, but few of these last as long a manufacturing production plant, and even in the most banal of entertainments there is an element of "creative interpretation". Individual artists and successful cultural organisations are able to give added value through variation, while sustaining a powerful "brand" identity that attracts investment and generates profits. As commercial products gain increasing added value through distinctiveness and niche marketing, business may learn from the cultural sector the techniques of variation and reinterpretation that keeps cultural production fresh. It is also true that as "symbolic goods" become increasingly important – goods whose aesthetic qualities, cultural associations and reflexive importance for the consumer give them a sign value that is more important than their use value – cultural consumption will acquire ever greater economic importance in the developed world, and business will need greater access to the skills in the symbol-creation and symbol-processing that is the artist's stock in trade.[51]

What culture will have to learn from business is a willingness to abandon long-established institutional forms and practices, to invest in new processes and set up new systems for generating them. It does not require the adoption of commercial values to learn the techniques of strategic planning, information management, communications and marketing, or to show a genuine commitment to research and development. Social capital is embodied in and by people, and for too long most artists, and those that work to support them, have been an exploited underclass, under-regarded and under-rewarded. Given the proper recognition that the Chancellor hints at, it is yet possible that what has been negatively inscribed as "the-right-to-fail" will be replaced by the positive will-to-succeed.

Notes

1. Mark H. Moore, *Creating Public Value: Strategic Management in Government*, Harvard University Press, 1995, p.93.
2. Sir George Cox, *The Cox Review of Creativity in Business*, H.M. Treasury, 2005.
3. Arts Council England, *Introducing the Cultural Leadership Programme*, 2006, p.8.
4. Sir George Holland, *Review of Management Training and Development in the Museums, Galleries and Heritage Sector*, Museum Training Institute, 1997, p.23.
5. For details, see Robert Hewison, "The Crisis of Cultural Leadership in Britain", *International Journal of Cultural Policy*, Vol. 10 no. 2, (2004), p.158.
6. Sara Selwood (ed), *The UK Cultural Sector*, Policy Studies Institute, 2001, p.253; National Endowment for Science, Technology and the Arts, *Creating Growth: How the UK can develop world class creative businesses*, NESTA, 2006, p.10.
7. Richard Sennett, *The Culture of the New Capitalism*, Yale University Press, 2006, pp 39-40.
8. Sennett, *op.cit.*, p.40.
9. See Robert Hewison and John Holden, *The Right to Art: Making Aspirations Reality*, Demos/VAGA , 2004.
10. Gavin Kelly, Geoff Mulgan, Stephen Muers, *Creating Public Value: An analytical framework for public service reform*, Cabinet Office Strategy Unit, 2002, p.15.
11. John Holden, *Capturing Cultural Value*, Demos, 2004; John Holden, *Cultural Value and the Crisis of Legitimacy*, Demos, 2006.
12. Robert Hewison and John Holden, *Challenge and Change: HLF and Cultural Value*, Demos/Heritage Lottery Fund, 2004.
13. Deborah Mattinson "The value of heritage – what does the public think?", in Kate Clark (ed), *Capturing the Public Value of Heritage: the Proceedings of the London Conference 25-26 January 2006*, English Heritage, 2006, pp 86-91.
14. Stephen Escritt, "Can Cultural Value Work?", unpublished research paper for Clore Leadership Programme, 2006, p.85.
15. Escritt, *op.cit.*, p. 85.
16. Moore, *op.cit.*, p. 10.
17. Moore, *op.cit.*, p.48.
18. Kelly *et.al.*, *op.cit.*, p.13.

19. Kelly *et. al.*, *op.cit.*, p.34.
20. BBC, *Building Public Value: Renewing the BBC for a digital world*, BBC, 2004, p.28.
21. BBC, *op.cit.*, p.29
22. Mark H. Moore, and Gaylen Williams Moore, *Creating Public Value Through State Arts Agencies*, Arts Midwest, State Arts Partnerships for Cultural Participation Program, 2005.
23. Arts Council England, *Report of the Peer Review*, 2005, p.v.
24. Arts Council England, *op.cit.*, p.15.
25. Arts Council England, *op.cit.*, p.vii.
26. Arts Council England, *op.cit.*, p.23.
27. Lord Redcliffe-Maud, *Support for the Arts in England and Wales*, Calouste Gulbenkian Foundation, 1976, pp 24-5.
28. Raymond Williams, "The Arts Council" (1979), in *Resources of Hope*, ed. Robin Gable, Verso, 1989, p.44.
29. Michael Power, *The Audit Society: Rituals of Verification*, Oxford University Press, 1995.
30. Emily Keaney, *Public value and the arts: Literature review*, Arts Council England, 2006.
31. Adrian Ellis, "Valuing Culture: A Background Note", position paper for "Valuing Culture" conference, National Theatre Studio, 2003, p.4.
32. Sir Peter Jonas, interviewed on "In Tune", BBC Radio 3, 28 August 2006.
33. For an account of Artangel, see Gerrie van Noord, *Off Limits: 40 Artangel Projects*, Artangel/Merrell, 2002.
34. AEA Consulting, *Serious*, Case Study for AEA Consulting, 2004, p.5.
35. For an account of the Regional Screen Agencies, see John Holden et al, *The Big Picture: The Regional Screen Agencies building community, identity and enterprise*, Demos, 2006.
36. Catalyst Arts, *The Thirst for Knowledge – Audience data in the arts*, ACE, Scottish Arts Council, Arts Council of Wales, 2003, p.4.
37. Catalyst Arts, *op.cit.*, p.9.
38. Catalyst Arts, *op.cit.*, p.7
39. Sara Selwood, "The Politics of Data Collection", *Cultural Trends* no.47, 2002, p.57.
40. Ricardo Blaug, Louise Horner and Rohit Lekhi, "Heritage, democracy and public value", in Kate Clark (ed), *Capturing the Public Value of Heritage: the Proceedings of the London Conference 25-26 January 2006*, English Heritage, 2006, p.24.
41. Sennett, *op.cit.*, p.64.
42. Christina Cameron, "Value and Integrity in cultural and natural heritage: from Parks Canada to World Heritage", in Kate Clark (ed), *Capturing the Public Value of Heritage: the Proceedings of the London Conference 25-26 January 2006*, English Heritage, 2006, p.75.
43. John Holden, *op.cit.* (2006), p.52.
44. Escritt, *op.cit.*, p.8.

45. Cameron, *op.cit.*, pp 76-7.
46. Moore, *op.cit.*, (1995), p.76.
47. Keith Grint, *Leadership: Limits and Possibilities*, Palgrave, 2005, p.38.
48. Grint, *op.cit.*, pp 46-7.
49. Grint, *op.cit.*, p.42.
50. Moore, *op.cit.*, (1995), p.17.
51. Robert Hewison, "The Arts in 2010", *Towards 2010: New times new challenges for the arts*, Arts Council England, 2000, pp 10-11.

Bibliography

AEA Consulting, *Serious*, Case Study for AEA Consulting, 2004

Beth Aplin, Kieran Cooper, Sarah Denner Brown, *The Thirst For Knowledge – Audience Data in the Arts*, Catalyst Arts, 2003

Arts Council England, *Report of the Peer Review*, 2005

Arts Council England, *Introducing the Cultural Leadership Programme*, ACE, 2006

Ricardo Blaug, Louise Horner and Rohit Lekhi, "Heritage, democracy and public value", in Kate Clark (ed), *Capturing the Public Value of Heritage: the Proceedings of the London Conference 25-26 January 2006*, English Heritage, 2006, pp 23-7

BBC, *Building Public Value: Renewing the BBC for a digital world*, BBC, 2004

Catalyst Arts, *The Thirst for Knowledge – Audience data in the arts*, ACE, Scottish Arts Council, Arts Council of Wales, 2003

Christina Cameron, "Value and Integrity in cultural and natural heritage: from Parks Canada to World Heritage", in Kate Clark (ed), *Capturing the Public Value of Heritage: the Proceedings of the London Conference 25-26 January 2006*, English Heritage, 2006, pp 71-78

Kate Clark (ed), *Capturing the Public Value of Heritage: the Proceedings of the London Conference 25-26 January 2006*, English Heritage, 2006

Sir George Cox, *The Cox Review of Creativity in Business*, H.M. Treasury, 2005

Adrian Ellis, "Valuing Culture: A Background Note", position paper for "Valuing Culture" conference, National Theatre Studio, 2003

Stephen Escritt, "Can Cultural Value Work?", unpublished research paper for Clore Leadership Programme, 2006

Keith Grint, *Leadership: Limits and Possibilities*, Palgrave, 2005

Robert Hewison, "The Arts in 2010",*Towards 2010: New times new challenges for the arts*, Arts Council England, 2000

Robert Hewison, "The Crisis of Cultural Leadership in Britain", *International Journal of Cultural Policy*, Vol. 10 no. 2, 2004

Robert Hewison and John Holden, *The Right to Art: Making Aspirations Reality*, Demos/VAGA , 2004

Robert Hewison and John Holden, *Challenge and Change: HLF and Cultural Value*, Demos/Heritage Lottery Fund, 2004

John Holden, *Capturing Cultural Value*, Demos, 2004

John Holden, *Cultural Value and the Crisis of Legitimacy*, Demos, 2006

John Holden et al, *The Big Picture: The Regional Screen Agencies building community, identity and enterprise*, Demos, 2006

Sir George Holland, *Review of Management Training and Development in the Museums, Galleries and Heritage Sector*, Museum Training Institute, 1997

Samuel Jones, *Talk Us Into It: Putting conversation into the heart of the public realm*, Demos, 2006

Emily Keaney, *Public value and the arts: Literature review*, Arts Council England, 2006

Gavin Kelly, Geoff Mulgan, Stephen Muers, *Creating Public Value: An analytical framework for public service reform*, Cabiniet Office Strategy Unit, 2002

Deborah Mattinson "The value of heritage – what does the public think?", in Kate Clark (ed), *Capturing the Public Value of Heritage: the Proceedings of the London Conference 25-26 January 2006*, English Heritage, 2006, pp 86-91

Mark H. Moore, *Creating Public Value: Strategic Management in Government*, Harvard University Press, 1995

Mark H. Moore, and Gaylen Williams Moore, *Creating Public Value Through State Arts Agencies*, Arts Midwest, State Arts Partnerships for Cultural Participation Program, 2005

National Endowment for Science, Technology and the Arts, *Creating Growth: How the UK can develop world class creative businesses*, NESTA, 2006

Michael Power, *The Audit Society: Rituals of Verification*, Oxford University Press, 1995

Lord Redcliffe-Maud, *Support for the Arts in England and Wales*, Calouste Gulbenkian Foundation, 1976

Gerrie van Noord, *Off Limits: 40 Artangel Projects*, Artangel/Merrell, 2002

Sara Selwood, "The Politics of Data Collection", *Cultural Trends* no.47, 2002

Sara Selwood (ed), *The UK Cultural Sector*, Policy Studies Institute, 2001

Richard Sennett, *The Culture of the New Capitalism*, Yale University Press, 2006

Raymond Williams, "The Arts Council" (1979), in *Resources of Hope*, ed. Robin Gable. Verso, 1989

DEMOS – Licence to Publish

THE WORK (AS DEFINED BELOW) IS PROVIDED UNDER THE TERMS OF THIS LICENCE ("LICENCE"). THE WORK IS PROTECTED BY COPYRIGHT AND/OR OTHER APPLICABLE LAW. ANY USE OF THE WORK OTHER THAN AS AUTHORIZED UNDER THIS LICENCE IS PROHIBITED. BY EXERCISING ANY RIGHTS TO THE WORK PROVIDED HERE, YOU ACCEPT AND AGREE TO BE BOUND BY THE TERMS OF THIS LICENCE. DEMOS GRANTS YOU THE RIGHTS CONTAINED HERE IN CONSIDERATION OF YOUR ACCEPTANCE OF SUCH TERMS AND CONDITIONS.

1. **Definitions**
    a   **"Collective Work"** means a work, such as a periodical issue, anthology or encyclopedia, in which the Work in its entirety in unmodified form, along with a number of other contributions, constituting separate and independent works in themselves, are assembled into a collective whole. A work that constitutes a Collective Work will not be considered a Derivative Work (as defined below) for the purposes of this Licence.
    b   **"Derivative Work"** means a work based upon the Work or upon the Work and other pre-existing works, such as a musical arrangement, dramatization, fictionalization, motion picture version, sound recording, art reproduction, abridgment, condensation, or any other form in which the Work may be recast, transformed, or adapted, except that a work that constitutes a Collective Work or a translation from English into another language will not be considered a Derivative Work for the purpose of this Licence.
    c   **"Licensor"** means the individual or entity that offers the Work under the terms of this Licence.
    d   **"Original Author"** means the individual or entity who created the Work.
    e   **"Work"** means the copyrightable work of authorship offered under the terms of this Licence.
    f   **"You"** means an individual or entity exercising rights under this Licence who has not previously violated the terms of this Licence with respect to the Work, or who has received express permission from DEMOS to exercise rights under this Licence despite a previous violation.
2. **Fair Use Rights.** Nothing in this licence is intended to reduce, limit, or restrict any rights arising from fair use, first sale or other limitations on the exclusive rights of the copyright owner under copyright law or other applicable laws.
3. **Licence Grant.** Subject to the terms and conditions of this Licence, Licensor hereby grants You a worldwide, royalty-free, non-exclusive, perpetual (for the duration of the applicable copyright) licence to exercise the rights in the Work as stated below:
    a   to reproduce the Work, to incorporate the Work into one or more Collective Works, and to reproduce the Work as incorporated in the Collective Works;
    b   to distribute copies or phonorecords of, display publicly, perform publicly, and perform publicly by means of a digital audio transmission the Work including as incorporated in Collective Works;
    The above rights may be exercised in all media and formats whether now known or hereafter devised. The above rights include the right to make such modifications as are technically necessary to exercise the rights in other media and formats. All rights not expressly granted by Licensor are hereby reserved.
4. **Restrictions.** The licence granted in Section 3 above is expressly made subject to and limited by the following restrictions:
    a   You may distribute, publicly display, publicly perform, or publicly digitally perform the Work only under the terms of this Licence, and You must include a copy of, or the Uniform Resource Identifier for, this Licence with every copy or phonorecord of the Work You distribute, publicly display, publicly perform, or publicly digitally perform. You may not offer or impose any terms on the Work that alter or restrict the terms of this Licence or the recipients' exercise of the rights granted hereunder. You may not sublicence the Work. You must keep intact all notices that refer to this Licence and to the disclaimer of warranties. You may not distribute, publicly display, publicly perform, or publicly digitally perform the Work with any technological measures that control access or use of the Work in a manner inconsistent with the terms of this Licence Agreement. The above applies to the Work as incorporated in a Collective Work, but this does not require the Collective Work apart from the Work itself to be made subject to the terms of this Licence. If You create a Collective Work, upon notice from any Licencor You must, to the extent practicable, remove from the Collective Work any reference to such Licensor or the Original Author, as requested.
    b   You may not exercise any of the rights granted to You in Section 3 above in any manner that is primarily intended for or directed toward commercial advantage or private monetary

compensation. The exchange of the Work for other copyrighted works by means of digital file-sharing or otherwise shall not be considered to be intended for or directed toward commercial advantage or private monetary compensation, provided there is no payment of any monetary compensation in connection with the exchange of copyrighted works.

c If you distribute, publicly display, publicly perform, or publicly digitally perform the Work or any Collective Works, You must keep intact all copyright notices for the Work and give the Original Author credit reasonable to the medium or means You are utilizing by conveying the name (or pseudonym if applicable) of the Original Author if supplied; the title of the Work if supplied. Such credit may be implemented in any reasonable manner; provided, however, that in the case of a Collective Work, at a minimum such credit will appear where any other comparable authorship credit appears and in a manner at least as prominent as such other comparable authorship credit.

5. Representations, Warranties and Disclaimer

a By offering the Work for public release under this Licence, Licensor represents and warrants that, to the best of Licensor's knowledge after reasonable inquiry:

i Licensor has secured all rights in the Work necessary to grant the licence rights hereunder and to permit the lawful exercise of the rights granted hereunder without You having any obligation to pay any royalties, compulsory licence fees, residuals or any other payments;

ii The Work does not infringe the copyright, trademark, publicity rights, common law rights or any other right of any third party or constitute defamation, invasion of privacy or other tortious injury to any third party.

b EXCEPT AS EXPRESSLY STATED IN THIS LICENCE OR OTHERWISE AGREED IN WRITING OR REQUIRED BY APPLICABLE LAW, THE WORK IS LICENCED ON AN "AS IS" BASIS, WITHOUT WARRANTIES OF ANY KIND, EITHER EXPRESS OR IMPLIED INCLUDING, WITHOUT LIMITATION, ANY WARRANTIES REGARDING THE CONTENTS OR ACCURACY OF THE WORK.

6. Limitation on Liability. EXCEPT TO THE EXTENT REQUIRED BY APPLICABLE LAW, AND EXCEPT FOR DAMAGES ARISING FROM LIABILITY TO A THIRD PARTY RESULTING FROM BREACH OF THE WARRANTIES IN SECTION 5, IN NO EVENT WILL LICENSOR BE LIABLE TO YOU ON ANY LEGAL THEORY FOR ANY SPECIAL, INCIDENTAL, CONSEQUENTIAL, PUNITIVE OR EXEMPLARY DAMAGES ARISING OUT OF THIS LICENCE OR THE USE OF THE WORK, EVEN IF LICENSOR HAS BEEN ADVISED OF THE POSSIBILITY OF SUCH DAMAGES.

7. Termination

a This Licence and the rights granted hereunder will terminate automatically upon any breach by You of the terms of this Licence. Individuals or entities who have received Collective Works from You under this Licence, however, will not have their licences terminated provided such individuals or entities remain in full compliance with those licences. Sections 1, 2, 5, 6, 7, and 8 will survive any termination of this Licence.

b Subject to the above terms and conditions, the licence granted here is perpetual (for the duration of the applicable copyright in the Work). Notwithstanding the above, Licensor reserves the right to release the Work under different licence terms or to stop distributing the Work at any time; provided, however that any such election will not serve to withdraw this Licence (or any other licence that has been, or is required to be, granted under the terms of this Licence), and this Licence will continue in full force and effect unless terminated as stated above.

8. Miscellaneous

a Each time You distribute or publicly digitally perform the Work or a Collective Work, DEMOS offers to the recipient a licence to the Work on the same terms and conditions as the licence granted to You under this Licence.

b If any provision of this Licence is invalid or unenforceable under applicable law, it shall not affect the validity or enforceability of the remainder of the terms of this Licence, and without further action by the parties to this agreement, such provision shall be reformed to the minimum extent necessary to make such provision valid and enforceable.

c No term or provision of this Licence shall be deemed waived and no breach consented to unless such waiver or consent shall be in writing and signed by the party to be charged with such waiver or consent.

d This Licence constitutes the entire agreement between the parties with respect to the Work licensed here. There are no understandings, agreements or representations with respect to the Work not specified here. Licensor shall not be bound by any additional provisions that may appear in any communication from You. This Licence may not be modified without the mutual written agreement of DEMOS and You.